I went in search of myself

Poetry for the end of days

ISBN: 978-0-6458057-0-3

Life screams relentlessly at us
Scraping and banging
Time's brutal rhythm
Marching steady as it comes
Bearing down in waves
Breaking against our sanity
We find combusted then
Elements, stirrings
Pieces left over
A game of circumstance
A knowledge waning
Interrupted faith
Where kinship is dispersed
And childless forfeited
Generations succumb
Their belonging irrevocably torn

In transgression we find
Measure of despair
Desperation wills its course
To breach ministry,
Justice, fury incumbent
Upon souls that dwindle
As the sun cuts a path
Across acres and homesteads
Mapping each module
Diminishing responsibility
Of care for growth and station
As fertility wilts
And age gives way to passing

When death creeps ineluctable
Joints twist and rupture
Fibrous being torn asunder
Hastened escape slips its juncture
When souls become moist
Carried on fragile wings
They bear not truly
As we hold on to delight while it lasts
Ultimate reality screams
Bearing down fast

As passion chokes reason
Dynamism of life melts into formless desire
Unceasing pressure builds monotonous
A drudgery enters and crushes
Yearning for quiet solemnity replaced
With perfidious clamour of lechery
Our dignity lost to base conscription
Consigned to faithless drive
Being to nightmarish emptiness
Where the soul cannot survive
Renewal only of flesh and form
Not a thing beyond the mire
Lost in demonic possession
Full of hatred, repugnant cascading
Entropic spiral, dominion punishing
A violent corruption of human devotion
To love and to treasure – instead
Truth collapsing, spirit expires

If it were custom to obey
Then one could shed the precepts
Of determined defiance
Opposed in all manners
As a spoilt microcosm
Thrown open to the macro
Summarised and crucified
When the counsel remains
But it is not that way
Though one forgets despite
All gates herding us
Directed to deign to defy
The edifice of nothing
As if it were something
Where what is left is already abandoned
Like a swirling blast
Mandated to rust

In the exhaustion of time
When all life is drained
The numbing pain of entropy
Shrouds in strangulation
A lifetime spent in obedience
Illogical steps followed
One after another
As circles traced
Compass of conformity
Enshrining our behaviour
Shared beginning
Ends split apart
Decayed and obliterated
Nothing left to salvage
Return to eternal stagnation
Corrupted being wilts
Like so many flowers in a vase

Death comes swiftly
To those who choose
A path of least resistance
Full of mercy, they obey
Confused, their master's chiding
Perfidious contemplation
Abandoned souls
Throw themselves in
Rhetoric convincing
Washes over them
Conscience ebbing out
Destructive contagion festers
A once proud people
Brought to nothing
Abandoned, molested
Laughing furiously
A broken chance
Howling decadence
Wrought upon them
Victims of self-doubt
Seeds of destruction sown
Malevolent forces
Crush our resolve
And seek to lay us low

Where sustenance fails us
The weak roll out their demands
And in punishing, feel rough contemplation
Edifying discriminatory lapses
Pulses of affinity wreaked upon
A wailing populace, a twisted consideration
In purest waters conceived
Distilled in arcane procedure
Distributed yet with foulest consequence
Intended to sustain life, uplift
Draws out instead havoc
Manically draining, contaminating
Our waters muddied now drain away
As thespian charlatans cavort before us
Try as we might to struggle,
To kick – to damage – we are lost –
To them, and us – drowned
On dry land now – evaporated
We lay desiccated and concussed

As death becomes
Faded reminiscence
Outlines decay behind the curtain
Draped over sunken liturgy
Gasping like bellows
Wind rushes through
Where contemplation is etched
Yet stone still erodes
And what is encased in concrete
Turns cancerous, consumes
Out of earth rises water
Flowing forth to drown the soul

Our sight is quenched
We breathe deeply
But it is not enough
An empty gulp
Shortness, a cut
Steady rhythm rests now
Struck alight
There's hope in the darkness
Of absence, confined
In waking we tremble
Reaching to find
The dead elude our grasp
And slipping into slumber
We cross the living path

Dry crack of whip
Shoots sharp and swift
Across the parched lip
Sparks of pain flash
As the gleam of light stutters
Flickering, soul departs
Wisdom lost, turned to ash
Our best we gave to this land
Barren and empty it left us
We turn to the heavens
To plead, decry a fate
We fight so hard to defy

Let not the weary rest
For they have not felt their burden long enough
They must suffer, dearly – through much pain
Ere their troubles stand level
With past encumbrances lashing our souls
Those flecks of cancerous becoming
Devouring all that is sweet to us
Hewn by time as if from rock
Dust settles about our deeds still now
But the story it tells is only of ruin
Of hunger and pious lamentations
Disease that rots both flesh and soul
Our wondrous feats of fevered fury
Fixed upon a moment in history
Drawing life from out of ages

When the hatred crystallises
Striking furiously outward
Compressed power exploding
And artifice is left behind
A truth is arrived at
Willingness to combat
Once tortured and forgotten hope
Now wrought upon the world
At war with itself
Distraught inclinations
Flexed across the emptiness
Wild fixation expands its tumult
And cascading labyrinths
Of captured humanity
Betray themselves in visions
Where decency hides
In nature folded tight
Showing all what may become
One to another, another to one

And if nothing awaits us
We cease then to pray
Hold off against deadly rumours
There comes faintly glowing
Morning sun, full of promise
When the earth turns its axis
And the march of time
Symbolises technical construction
Drumming calculations in rhyme
To understand we must process
Watch wearily in focus
As our world is spun out
Through a critical focus
Yet despite our conception
This world covers us still in deception
And our mark misses its place
So we see edifices crumbling
Beneath the façade
Where dreams have died

In every foundered search
There lies a strange knowing
Deep beyond the limits of the body
Travels lithe a beaming motion
To find the measure of the soul
Our struggles fruitless yield
Not bounty of imagination, beginning
Forms of movement travel wide
Over barren wastes, dusty foes
Encounter foreign, our core
Unlocked in depth of sands
Eroding, channelled raw
In plains of infinite silence we see
Palms of greeting raised beyond the sea
Of spring in welcome, thought arrived
Departed again – fleet shifting
Sands combine to form rapport
With time, our souls melt
Slide into desert abyss

Separate to bind
In togetherness find
Moment of renunciation
Other symptoms
Ill-defined disclosure
Consequences brightened
Spark of disavowal
Omen pointed
Coagulated dreaming
Stirred through memory
A portion founded
Across the even path
Where remote channels
Desiccated by difference
Furrowed in cooperation
Empty now
Only shattered vials

Souls in decline, matching their trap
Of language, understanding faulted
Through means we witness
Spawning new and feted
These gestures decay
Our evidence expelled
Features sloping, eyes betray
A loss of explanation
Forgotten memories unheard
For time's breach is abandoned
Movement abides, thought remains
What we feign to broach
We cannot hear, nor say

Crush the scrapped consensus
Into mounds of limitless choosing
Undone in memory, learning turns
Taken further, artful discerning
Left not to bring us wisdom
But to rob and straight pursue
Inquiry altered subtle, true
Behaviour twisted light
Knave adjunct to, thought, clues
To living, opened not with keys
Digested thorough, naked peace
What can reveal itself
Composed in reverie, fevered interruption
Come what may, if we but knew

Only the contemptible remain
In forms multiplying and removing
They trace their idle viciousness
Not in firm conviction, but reactive
Spurned by phantoms past
Appetite for redemption
As a salve for their misgiving
Parting insolent lips to purge
Junction of being thrown open
In pursuit of this divide to close
A pain must be drawn forth
But instead of slow revelation
Offset, displaced their suffering distorts
Cast onto others it drains souls
Into nothing, self-abhorred

Deception bridges corruption
Where wisdom goes to die
In a casket of desperation
We scramble to catch a wisp
Of thin air rising forth
Out from what we destroy
Alloyed in action we form
A cryptic nothing in siphon
Of missed observation
Conspicuous through presence
Worked into absence
Of opposites in transformation
We lose our senses
As transposition augments
Decay of things left
Behind our disposition
We carry them away

Broken clusters of sediment
Cracked and parted in pans
Baked hard and brittle
Under sun of decay
Resumption of duties
Looming over day
Flurry parts – through
Escape in change
Only to mark again
Echo skew, eyes from
Shade to brilliance
Blinded, refused

Gorge our thoughts upon the day
More to prove – and to gain
That there is something to profane
Though constant ringing out
Doubt and confusion, fevered spout
Daily play consume again
As children, greedy for discipline
Eschew the lesson, run – free
Barter doctrine, liberty
Illusory choice, locked in curse
Of vain repetition, pointless dearth
In opinions find an emptiness
As in the belly, no surprise
A hollow nothing there abides

Resonance of being echoes our sentiment
Of past confusions, rendered clear
Where realignment shuffles across
A vast chasm of changes
Yawning across the ocean of time
Its spotted circumference peels back
The shudders of intuition, aghast
At all things that come to pass
Through variance, counter-thrust
Race to attune in perfect harmony
In haste defeated – a lapsed release
Of hatred against stillness
Where prosperity reigned
A card slipped under, a boon spilled over,
But the striving for sublation
Integration of negation
Produces yet a leftover unaccounted
Plaintive dissonance again chimes
And passing once more into foreboding
The answer comes resounding back

The forever blue sky booms across our sights
And knowing in our comprehension of this time
A silent nothing abides, tucked in fright
Of waking to a knowledge, failing to climb
To that spot in nature's abiding light
Pure, untried with such words and rhyme
That which is, or distinguishing, right
What's asleep in fury, climbs towards the sublime
Countenanced by oblivion, ending with time

Driven like the rain
Slashing a path
Through rhythm of emptiness
Clattering down in a maelstrom
Of blows struck heavy
On backs and limbs
Until brutality pushes
Beasts ever further
Under they go
Into mists of unbroken bounds
Spirit sequestered
Stashed away
Where no beauty resides
Lest it be crushed in the fray

Jewels spark from on high
Reflecting totality of bliss
Without great purpose of light
Shine in eternity, cascading flight
Would that deeper meaning present
Or fade to nothing, bereft of sentience
Being without, what could they become
If shattered negation would form into one
Amalgam of forces, radiant power
Gleam in the eye of heaven, they reach
For tomorrow's vestigial hour

Are you able to hear? What they are saying
What? - Absent fear.
Of a mourning, says their witness
But would you portend?
The presence, in absence of the same
Can be a delightful omission
As follows reluctance of sound
Deaf hear as you speak
That loss of content, falling down
Drops beneath the presentation
Framing nothing now - empty halls

Expecting much of nothing little
Movement tracking out in ripples
Parts the mountains, courses torn
Explore faint traces deftly worn
Lingers on in chimes unknown
Baked and crumbling flecked in stone
Variation merging time as one
Dimension flows, becomes undone

Arcs of blunt humility
Stream in stippled corruption
Lulled towards face of change
Slinking through open fields
Lined with sentiment it cripples
Abandoned monstrous overture
Dawning ancient horizon
Awakens treated word
Renewal in repetition
Could the burning mitre
Cut across our plains?
Dream of new deliverance
Now left without name
Find in endless daybreak
That self-same breaking day
Inured to the condition
Every cockcrow yawns the same

Where the way weaves its spokes
Into ash, felt in waves rolling flat
High above common course
Yolks us through oblivion's track
Slipping, at odds we associate
With constant, nagging -
Chancing nothing, harbouring fate.
Sails then against persistence, snaps
Meeting now seems strange again
As every day drifts far away
So we come to prize the pen
Capture that which leads astray
Act and speak as opposite
In darkness moving sluggish mute
Hollowed out, thought somnolent
Transposed against path acute

Preference slipped from out of sight
Junctures opened by the prying
Substance betrayed under night
Unconscious blemish deftly lying
Comes in fits, leaves us stark
Robbing perception, transfer mark
Crossing inception, trace the capture
Explication draining, endure fracture
Hearing forces, alter conception
Despondent rumble, effort redouble
Breaking through opaque perception
Learning now – reality uncoupled

From death emerges
A new sequence
Partitioned dissonances
Wafted gently towards waking
Where a pantheon resides
Magnificent, imposing
Yet humble in its beauty
Revived significance
All things retain
A whisper of their force
Extorted from sleep
Blank immanence
Meaning nothing
We start and fade

Ashes of dreams scorched in requital
Of all that is and would be
Fire for all things
In waves its heat pulses, lofty churning
Air cracks and whips about
As gold loses form, and goods erupt
Infinity opens its jaws
And Satan's tempest throttles forth
Incandescent power hammering
All things
Caught in vapour, heat consumes
The earth, and gold and goods
And all that ever lived passes
Through the conflagration
Out in torrid air
Nothing saved, empty doom

When the stench of failure
Leers up at us
Encroaching all around in a thick mist
Shrouding and confusing
As steam rising from a vent
Our souls burst open
And the sinister reality
Lays its burden upon us finally
Where we lie now
Not in purgatory
But descended
Into a hell of being
Bereft of all belonging
And awash with decay
We sink below life itself
Finding only emptiness
And the limitless nothing

I went in search of myself
To try to find the patterns of identification
Lurched into contemplation's crushing hold
Squeeze sweet angst with wrings of turning
Folded twist of burnt despair
I sought myself here somewhere
But could not open life to show me
What was missing hidden, lithe it snatched
From grasp blind reaching, fearing never
To be held in place, nor present in mind
Would that these secrets of identifying
Want of being, to declare – that moving,
Changing, growing whisper proffered to me
From breach of nothing, emerging fair
Lost now again to time's negation
And on I stumble in foreign air
In time that cannot tell me why
It should pain me more to die
Than live in world of desperate guile
Trampled under force of life
Never follow that but which increases yield
To me that sanctuary of destruction
Deliverance must find a way
In arriving at that restitution
Not of fund but of living
Return to me that final age
Of being noble and sincere
That I could live again with peers

Share of what we have conquered, obtained
Grasping towards the ultimate, our aim
What could become of that open account
Thought in expansion, bridged to surmount
That private possession - revealed, incarnate
Lived out, public, in marvellous faith
Returned in kind by reflected exchange
Objectified process turned solid, alive
Absorbed into consciousness, as unity arranged

Learn not to understand
Traditions left over ramble
Into precepts of vigour
Giving themselves authority
Rushing to renew a lost aspect
Culture slips through our fingers
Rends weak flesh from soft formations
Desperation giving way, lost occupations
What would we take, were strength there to rise
Forgive not our own weakness, learn to despise
Those short manoeuvres, cheap happening
Come to understanding, advance to the fight

With the forgotten shards of time
Fracturing in brilliant thunder claps
Of shattered solidarity, splintering
Chaos of destruction in forms
Meted out in morsels of one
Becoming, listen to its merging
Harbinger of all that is
Coalescence of the whole
Comes in drops, it sleets, it pours
Drowning out the rhythm of being
The sturdy semblance soaked
Swollen, twisted raw
Many now one, in sullen amalgam
Never sundered more

To know and to think
All that is and would become
Through nothing belonging, well
To mind first utterance
Climb softly toward deciphered crust
Of crumbled time, broken twice
Once for supper, once for us
Encrypted matter decayed again
Specks of dwindled substance
Dotted across the pan of reason
As able judges sit and mutter
What of the telling, only chatter
Inclined to ruminate of man
His deeds, knowledge – plans
But ask for deeper meaning find
Open meandering through mine
Own thought lost, wander further still
Chasing integration of one will
To keep accordance with our pact
With wisdom shouldered on motive's back

When tufts of infinity sprout in the distance
Gentle contemplation may be interrupted
Through moments, gusts of change
Though time rolls slowly, not announcing itself
But moving methodically, disclosing truth.
So when a vacuum rips through the landscape
And nature's dull magnitude permeates
Hollowed out, devoid of substance
As life escapes in trails of ember
Billowing violence pummels onwards
And we must quench its insanity
Its restless momentum of doom
Or succumb to evil – where all is lost
Cities, homes, culture, lives
We cannot allow it to flourish
Lest our entire civilisation be lost

Speak with understanding
Fast hold comprehending
A shared judgement of our law
Protect and uphold in presence of more
Than cities, lives, unveiling
Essence in divination
Call of nourished explication
Dancing out of revelation
Human, force, prevailing
As willing enough for them
Doing as it will, suffice us
To unite, citizens then

The order for all things
Sets and congeals
Fixed in lines
Primed and wedged
Hard into the passage of being
Afforded certain order
In time's accordance
As change augurs
Necessity of fate
Driving inevitably
Past what draws us
To conclude the outcome
Performing ready
We act out our ambition
Grail to prize
Seeking, boring through
Breached momentum
Worlds locked in motion
Crashing askew

One seeks knowing most
Through night becoming day
Teacher of recognition
Flight of expansion, turning out
Progression spirals, curves about
Our mind in restless motion
Of deceiving notion held plain
Emerging through devotion
To research, to mine
A thought inside the ear
Of God whispering secret revelation
Drilling sharp
As man falls down to earth
Heart beating 'gainst soil
Sand lost in crumbling
Time of full and bounteous growth
Appear again
To us as in our dreams
The unity of confusion
Pointing – moving through bright streams

Were it to come to this
When all beauty is cloaked
In shadow of foreboding judgement
When the wisest are shouted down
Conquered by quantity
We race to the archive
Feet padding swift, true
Lines split and fray
Knowledge for keeping
Finds us lost, even deeper
Removed from the border
Of time's steady dominion
Shocks quaking through
Souls lost, entombed
Mausoleum of degeneration
Envelopes and crowds
Forces heavy, as if inexorable
Our masked determination

Where understanding fails us
Shocks surge up and through
Sense of isolation, listless
Life drifts across the outlet
Bound for the sea
Motion lilting swells
And bound to land yet
Reason draws us back
Lures us into its fold
Even as we slip by
Channelled beyond the break
Away from the heavy clatter of the many
Chanting worthless banalities
While our wits have already failed us
We are at peace, at last
We who eluded those
That remained to watch the farce

And as the spike of dominion crowds us
Water trickles on the panes
Icy and with bitterness laced
Our hands shrouded, not by mists
But cut and split by elements
Ravages of earth and weathered days
Cumbersome in their bearing
Scrapes that dot the landscape
Bodies wearied, sink in the mud
Figures in passing, latched and primed
When a sound delivers execution
Excitement shivers aloft
Emboldened by struggle
The fool holds sway for an instant
Until accounted, crumbles

What were these things
Granted to us, bestowed by time
With patience of slow being
Fraught meaning angled from divine
Where currents in passing
Push through manifested liquid sky
Descending from billows
Suffocating tragedy, balming essence
As leaders abandon
Like so many frail husks
Shedding public shells
Running for shelter
From fallout, from ash
Of burning indignation
Now will you know that name
Justice – let it ring out its fiery rebuke

To hide in the desert of the living
Concealed in plain sight
Benevolence flounders
Where manifested indiscretion
Falls as tears in one's cups
And that ease of being eludes us
As we fight to be chaste
Disciplined and moral
While the erosion of our souls
Proceeds as inevitably
Whether concealed or open
Our faith must congeal
Harden against our age
To bolster and lift the spirit
Beyond the vulgar stuff
That constitutes our days

We share the green vision of a cracked future
Crisp and smooth with skin incision
Drip of fading tack in caution
Bump in fresh aspect, elision
Meaning switched, open schism
Between what is shared and what
Corrupts, think in parting we commune
Desire union with all in common
Yet lined fable of amnesia drifts us
Toward a trickle of emptiness
Incumbent upon our souls
The nothing of evanescent sound
Punctures determined positing
As core of being fades

In the contemplation runs
Error of calculation, desperation
Etches furiously caustic
Pained gasps exasperating
A monument stands untouched
Discipline and honour gave rise to this
Where desecrated clasps hang
A memory, faded
Channelled into history
Where passion reigns
And ministry is drained
Into obsolescence once more
Where time's burden collapses
And a new figure emerges
Foreboding dark changes
Patterns coalesce into vengeance
Failed crusades descend
Power recedes
Where confluence of circumstance
Arises new and pure
You shall be defeated
Do not dare to challenge our order
For reason and truth will prevail
Through whatever means we avail

Speak to what is true in finding
Wisdom creeps and startles us
Binding leaves in wicks about the place
Filled with duration to infinity
Occupying fragility, choking bundle
Of lumbered wax, melted truss
Supported nature, according true
Perceiving excellence we cleave
The sight of weakened terraces
The landscape of our passions
Draining, floats away
The bumble of sweet dilapidation
Transformed into a new convent
Of blood and suffering, renewal guide
Power of moulding turned inside
Out of settlement, heritage slides
Onwards, as they howl
Of wind and conversation
Where acting well is greatest truth

In dimensions of abstraction
There frays a loose thread
Sanity unwinding, blessings defined
Some progress for shared accordance
Where the realised mind awaits
In plumes of desperation
A fog shrouds the maze
Of our tortured circumstance
Needled sharp defining
As pines rake, climbing
Empty over plots
Of shared conflict
Combined to pass
Ordained in permanence
Our burden of justice
Heralds war for all times

Let them hang for their crimes
Deserving to the last man
They posture and sham
Thinking only of avarice
Let none forward strive
Only maximise, justify
Existing order replicates
Its pillars radiate
Glory founded smouldering
Among rubble of culture
Driven to fragment
Remnants of a city
Left to others, lost to us
And in the choking dust explosion
Detritus smothers even rubble
As youth are left to build
What elders allowed to crumble

When the filth is washed away
Swept from the mire to eternity
Solemn voices will pronounce
That mystery enunciated like a breath
In water cleansed, our faithlessness purged
Bathe in ignorance no more
Come forth and announce
We are arrived, must not be denied
As the delight rises amongst us
Substantiated being, constant hold
Our bonds shall not break
For together we strive
Undoing ruination of an empty world
Without meaning or substance
No tears will be shed
When our flag is unfurled
And the intonation of the funeral rite
Wafts across the West

In the infinite stages of passing
Pillars morph into stumps
Age of giants crumbled
Remains propped, as a burden
To the new found insolence
Brazen disregard for heritage
Culture lost in time's descending
And so aurora comes despite
Struggles we meet, forlorn we fight
Yet with the dawning comes renewed
Our call to action, life to pursue
In the afterglow of eternity
We rekindle the heat of our passions
Uphold the old order, let time resume

If we pray in muted tones
For a word consoling, bones
Meanings, pairs in rapid motion
Avalanche confine the mind
Encrust our desolation to bind
Our voices unheard in devotion
As child to parent we listen
But unknowing now we christen
The nightmare seamless notion
Fear of rupture, where bonds contain
Now melt away, willingness feign

At the end of days
When all is lost
And rhythm fades
Nothing remains
Soul stripped back
Naked and cold
Essence lost
As time unfolds
Where fury would hope to grow
Instead lies empty, broken
Defeated shell
As crooked paths wind
Towards the wheel
Where time loses meaning
No life is fostered here
Only death, a vacuum
Yet we must enter
Dealt these cards
Our hand is forced to play
For sundered from life
In desolation we find
Resonance of fellow spirits
Effort to become
Finally sound of mind

One is knowing, like and who
Nature of the thing revealed
Becoming – mapped new
To steer the course afforded
All that verges into view
Plan of broad agenda
Days of creation, guided few
Joyous accompaniment
Resonates across our land
Imbued with knowledge
We demand, a kindness
Shared refrain, pleasant accrue
Our focus and hardship alike
So that we may conquer
Draw our power
Cover the way
For we know it too

In deed and word we forge our bond
Acquire what did once belong
Fated before centuries
Hard won in trust, fulfilling need
To wisdom driven, loving know
Many storied obstacles merged
Through multiplicities smouldering glow
Submerge in substance clearing
Emerging brilliant gleaming
Clasping founded glorious mastery

Rise to the fight, strike well
Our enemies in mind
Against nothing, define
Give credence to no one
Not now, before time
But soak the ground
In ribbons of life
Spun out like crimson drops from the vine
Where the snake catches taste
Droplets in dust
Rivulets coagulate
As the steam rises
From souls expiring in trust
For they came to rally
To cover their walls
But the weakness lay within
Beneath their pores
Drowned in trespass
Forsaken laws
Judge not our conquering
That which corrupts
Can never be restored

There is in hidden power
A seductive attunement
Program for the cause
Kernel of truth manifests
Gestation submerged
Smooth patterns link
Minds and souls
Where unity breathes yet
Life into forms belonging
Not to surface guardians
But to the underground
Tectonic provocation
Lights emerge
Eyes pierce fissures
As in unison
Our glory returns

When the dust settles on this parched world
Rains rolling on a broken metropolis
Empty plains housing no crops
Only filled with the lies of progress
Encountered peripheral, our invented fate
Those that swore to them lie strewn now
Over the hills and fields, in the streets
For justice has been wrought
And in the twisted rubble of our cities
A hammering can still be heard
The sound of judgement
Of pitiless scorn we have heaped
On all those that would betray mankind
Sold for a fair price, to the highest bidder
We will destroy them, now and forever
No traitor shall survive our law

And if we honour those
Whom we held dear
Will God not smile upon us?
Will they not look down and cheer?
Or are we lost?
Strewn out and bloodied
Across the field
Where battle was drawn
Lines were held and broken
A tremendous tumult thundered
Acrid taste of agony
Left lingering sickly in the air
Now emptiness reigns
Void to be filled with lamentations
Of pain wrought by men
On his fellows in kind
But remember sweet pacifist
What we fought for
And why we must
Lest there be no fellow kind
Left over
After so long in indolence
In forfeit and decay
In loss and destruction
Without a drop of blood spilled
Remember
What we have already lost
And why we must not let it come to pass
That we lose all that remains

When we rise up
Becoming
Surging forth in waves
Abandoning our graves
To rise again and survey
Treasures of sparkling life
Bathed in shining glory
Remembering mankind's story
Awake to the day
Where we are our choices
And owning what we do
We make our world this way

What with our patterns, our curdling mirth
Judgement and deception, foolhardy birth
Giving rise to new things, envious ruse
Of day to day living, in breath we exude
Willingness, expectation, declaring our claim
To a piece of that science, worked out – fairly
Yet roundabout and haphazard we lie and lurch
Through our share of misgivings and fortune
Too much, worry nothing, ill informed – too soon!
But when the illusions of sun disappear,
Scars of living accrue in our ears
Manifested in loss – age wearying foul
Disqualified and tossed – aside
From spectres of longing – of what could become
Dispatch our reasons, our hope, all done.
Watch now as opening, with feet stepping near
Ceaseless progression of privation, despair
In knowing now what we profess to do
Change little, if any feature as dues
Accrue and lather to thick sickening paste
Distorting and concealing what's left of our faces
Embarked from sweet memories in song
Full of optimism, blessed attitudes
Withered by marching we now testify
Thought has us beaten – inwards we try
To shake the persistence, but soon we are through
Left now to crush and expel this muse

And when the sun sets –
When the day bleeds no more
Our eyes and souls
Ruptured specks
Bubbling conviction
Flung in proposal of being
Duration, existence
Passing through light
Where spores trundle up
Block and cloud
Haze filters becoming
As roused notion
Holds up its head
As if to nod
Acknowledgement, day
As night infiltrates

If the cataract of reason
Were to cleave the infinite
Men stand unrecognised
Wrestling with doubt
Hounded by the other
Thrown into confusion
Baying for recompense
Alms awaiting
Stretched to multiply
As dogs bark
Wind howls
And we forfeit our chance

We sleep again
As the night folds in
Dragged down to reality's pause
A moment, fragmented
Where struggle ceases
Labour is absolved
Yet still we work
To form the bonds
With waking souls
Transition in rupture
Brought forth in pulses
A disruption pursues
Ripple of continuity
As the world rises
And history comes to pass

In the immaculate glow of youth
Shines a bright knowing love
Where life dominates
Leaps forth exuberant
And passion envelops, throws
Wanton proliferation of being
Out into action
Worlds are conquered
Deeds transposed into halls
Of ageless divinity
Where memory sleeps
Sound in the knowledge
Tradition prevails
Our community will stand
In waking and sleep
Perpetual... the same

In moments of passing
Fleeting essence leaps out to us
Clasping at the seconds
Drawn taught across time's surface
Worked through history's knots
A portion of life
Doled out in name
Formed in being
Expanding without limit
Measured to capacity
Overtaking now
It pulses densely
Conversing internally
Words muffled sound
Louder building
Life here proclaimed

Were that some elements
Vanquished in time's impetus
Could linger on
Defining through discordance
Fabled harmony
For there can be no peace
No resolute justification
Eternal cessation
Movement abides in change
And there it stays
Thriving complexity
Halting in conflict
Holding patterns of motion
Drive combines and destroys
Frayed edges of being
Vanish in the noise

Pulsing mind races
Cycles generate
A life in time
Intervals collapsing
Onto themselves in formation
Nature returning
Engendered time
Lapse of strata
Where years linger
A longing forms
For progeny to continue
As in a sound
Perpetuated through language
We determine our being
In song and devotion

In early hours of dawning
Folds of light stagger forth
A concertina of affirmation
Berates our soul into action
So waking, we plot our daily course
As strident, mining thought
Discloses our condition
We strangle the partition
Where life divided eludes us
A creeping substance
Under surface of being
Pulses outward
And a denial turns
Reciprocated sentiment
As report goes out
Unknown though its course

Sentinel of cycles
Determined wrath of becoming
Seer of changes – all
Seasons past and future
Present shining, loops conforming
Move in torrent looming
Above and out of time
As if a motion clouded
Passage of being itself
Through fields of history
Harvest premonition
From out of tangled bramble
To pick apart the meaning
Of birth and death – if able

River of changes – flow
Through day and night
From deserts form oceans
Transfer solid into motion
Of becoming – notion
Absolute, encompassed
Totalised reality, clasped
Sure in our clutches
As being remains, shifts, departs
Emerges again, alike, yet new
Points to its elements
Sublated, see true
Manifold descendants
Impart the view
Faint coloured perception
Trickled time pursue

And the changes come
Dispersed through wandering
As eyes become heavy
Emptied of thought
Dreams coalesce
Upon the mind's vision
Notion of a world
In stasis, brought level
Accompanied by constant
Hum of living time
Where being rests
And life becomes mine

Waking now to sound of turning wheels
Crushing stone, fruit of the alley cobble
Twisted levels, dribbling faint as caution
Remnants linger creviced behind
Sleeping away in cornered world
Private each belonging true
Spurned by others, who dormant knew
Sharing only that which drops
Down upon the cluttered spots
Through cracks it glitters
Naming earth in turn
Awake at last commune again
Sweet salve of patience
Sigh of dawn in breaking

When one could account for more
As when earth has come to rest
Night's studded cloak
Wraps and weighs
On souls and conscience
As if with meaning draped
So many lives tucked away
In slumber and in graves
Now that piteous heat has snuck
'Round the corner
Left residual glowing
Still laughter mocks
Scorns our weariness
Lights fading – drop

Mortal substance – abides
As one seeks to grasp
It scatters – subsides
Again to gather
Form our resolve
Stable aspire, to reach – approach
Dissolves the condition
Departing once more
Yet semblance divides
Trace here – no more
That which is left
Cannot be captured
Set firm – unmoved
For the world lures it out
Into changes, forms
Of contrast disintegrated
Shifting time – deform

In the firelight we find a solace
Peace not of our signification
But of stimulated generation
Heat, in flame – although we cower
From its vigour, yet we are drawn
To its solemn power
Revealing energy of destruction
Breaking down, concerted function
Given over to logic of construction
Forging declaration, conceal not
Our inclination, to consume,
To hunt, destroy, devour
All that remains beneath
Hours of longing, hours they chime
Riven by consequence
Honed in pyre of time

Where the question arises
Dawn finds its limit
In revealing the border
Opposites closing, rings of triumph
Running luminous in gardens
Of herbs and weeds
Densely cropping forms
Yearning for one
Yield of evening
Ward our process
Against the even tide
And watch, knowing
We stretch out, labyrinth –
Crossing, divide

Faintly as the sunrise looms
Morning now for birds resumes
Speak to us yet passing by
All meaning lost, they blot the sky
What can these creatures pose to say
When softly, faintly glide away
On wings of vapour, churning light
The heavens unfolded in our sights
Bereft of reason, cannot hear
Neither can their chatter endear
A mind to muddy, striking lapse
Not sight nor sound - worlds collapse

Set apart, in time we dive
Thriving absence in peculiarity
Hum of vertigo, greeting lost
Account heard softly from afar
Drifting recognition would reveal
A thought ingrained in its appeal
To solace, to semblance solitary
Sense of withdrawal in all of those
Souls now wiser for the loss
A revelling tuned to be recalled
But reverberation hollow rings
As being fleets in time's pause

Never ceasing days of toil
Perpetual struggle embroils
Our thoughts and deeds
In vain again we bleed
The day is lost, fades away
Home we trundle, humbly pray
To find a difference, now and then
But tasks repeat, though we repent
For what we've done
We do not know
Offended, whom – friend or foe?
Has God passed judgement?
Still softly moan
This weariness, our soul imbibes
Incessant beginning
Day prescribes
The same again – until we die

Winter of a thousand years
Descend upon us now
Put out this conflagration
In summer of despair
Flames lap the edges of our sanity
As we spiral to destruction
Nerves frayed, conscience gone
Hellish streets beckon us down
Towards the Great Year
Where floods will drown
Hatreds conquered
Throes convulsing
Death is near
Renewal is here

To reverse the fire from the sea
First we must break the bond of vigilance
And let our gaze drop to the core
In storm's throes of agony going
Intrepid follow the earth
Into the depths, void of ocean
Darkness clouding, hidden even
To lightning strike
And crack earth's dry bones, to flood
Streams converging
Confronting our hope
Struck as strange to us
Ringing of the rock clash
As waves crush devotion

In their thousands they rained
From sky to the limit of beyond
Turning about to front the sea of the many
Faces shimmering ephemeral
Periphery wanes as edges sag
Crippled by time and worn
Caress of deadly refraction
As light splinters in waves
When space bends accompaniment
And mirages hide our decay
Ultimate eddies past

Rush of water beams
Punching through the snow
Icy sparkle gleaming
Iridescent glow
As other aqua ebbs
Rivers wash below
Shifting steps now teeming
With kaleidoscopic contradiction
Punctuating knowing
Interrupted flow
And still the other looms
Contaminating thought
Where – upon the empty silhouette
A doubt seeps through
We lose our senses
Stepping false
Slip and feel the water's chill

Soar unto the stars
We float in finding
Reconfigured crystal skies
Blackened by time
Faded from life
Lost in the momentum of being
Incendiary flashes, breath of light
Mist of immanence, emanate
From imminent merging
One, with two
Three forms emerging, shining through
What if we could see, as the ancients could
The slim moments of substance
Revealed in time with precious release
Unclose to us mythical potence
Being, becoming, repose

If life were kindled as flame bright
In measures teeming, flickering,
Spritely licking, toward heaven it wraps its prongs
Around fuel for disintegration, now fading out
For what man has made must come to cease
In torrents of fury it finds its release
Of life unbridled, from death undone
The drive to destruction is that which will come
Order we might, what is right and good
But when we measure what is and not,
What may be or become, no one can help us
No man overcome, the spires of peril,
Flame wrapped – hurtling through, the
Making of all that was to stay one
Burns to the ground again to renew
The struggle from wisps of ash consumes
To erupt and devour once more

Pouring forth from the ruins of substance
Shattered being lies strewn across the sea
Earth scattered nameless upon its pulsing shores
Disaster metes out measured nothing
As cause runs softly away, trickling condensation
Caught on crags of elemental stone
Clustered amongst the pattern of refinement
Sand crisp and dry crackles as wind rolls
Over the banks and the tufts of sway
Cropped sediment settling baked as bone
Cut the same from whence it was combed
Stripped back and multiplied, left to mill
Into dust of eternity, grist for the will

In the fullness of evocation
A solemn tone rings out
Closing in, tracing spiral
Bridging light – bright eruption
Drawn from time's shadow
Uplifts yawning focus
As from the dark
Energy renews, captured
Brought through –
Fastened to the infinite
Its eminence transfixed
From wandering tracked
Suspended nexus
Purifies perception
All knowing

Death sweeps forth all in its wake
As birth for eternity, intermingling
Fragments of fire and air
The dying out of light
Forms dust, ebbing out over horizons
In multitudes it fades
Slips through time's fingers
Leaves us with a fleeting nothing
Moments of pain vanishing
Into remnants of our lives
This is what remains
A grain, a whisper
A flicker in the darkness
A pause in the infinite

Beyond a sober resentment
Transcribed through origin
Opens up an abyss
Where the emptiness of being
Screams silent, relentless
As perception is shrouded
No vale will lift to reveal
Only the void remains
A great yawning nothing
Through which we aimlessly stumble
Unknowing, souls downcast
And if ever we are to escape
Our eyes must turn heavenward
For man's dominion is but short lived
Ephemeral, laced with fragility
Frayed and torn
As life's curtain is drawn

In divinity we seek what we cannot find
Leap into chaos, search to define
Terms of engagement with world confined
To pulses, washing grief from our souls
Doubt wrenches, cleansing ruptured
Purpose courses through the sky
But here on earth we squabble and mutter and die
Fumes and dust spew heavy, solidified
Cast as fate would carry – hide now
In ignorance, or chance; where no one decides
Yet abiding in light and vapour
Clouds and blue distance
Is the all determining, demystified

When God speaks to us he reveals
Not the judgement of the finite
Nor the harrowing multiplicity of time
For lodged in his word is objectivity
Idea manifested, perfectly attuned
Formed of reality, its totalising universality
Renders with just hand the measure
Of all that is, all that has been
Where the infinite plays its game
What is meant to be – is.
To seek what is good and fair
Is to pursue all things as declared
Known and mapped by time
Labour of cognition renders to us
Knowledge, undiscriminating,
For all is just and right and – there

www.ingramcontent.com/pod-product-compliance
Lightning Source LLC
Chambersburg PA
CBHW020328010526
44107CB00054B/2022
* 9 7 8 0 6 4 5 8 0 5 7 1 0 *